Shortcuts to

making hard choices easy

Other titles in the series:

Shortcuts to

making hard choices easy

Gael Lindenfield

Thorsons

Thorsons
An Imprint of HarperCollins*Publishers*
77–85 Fulham Palace Road
Hammersmith, London W6 8JB

The Thorsons website address is: www.thorsons.com

and *Thorsons*
are trademarks of
HarperCollins*Publishers* Ltd

First published by Thorsons 2002

1 3 5 7 9 10 8 6 4 2

© Gael Lindenfield 2002

Gael Lindenfield asserts the moral right to be
identified as the author of this work

A catalogue record of this book is
available from the British Library

ISBN 0-00-710053-1

Printed and bound in Great Britain by
Omnia Books Ltd, Glasgow

To Sue Marvel Denton

With love and admiration for the way you have strived to make the best choices in testing circumstances.

Acknowledgements for the

Shortcuts Series

First, thanks again to all the people who have so openly shared their struggles with me. I hope that you will be pleased that the wisdom I gained from your difficult experiences has been constructively channelled into these Shortcut strategies.

Secondly, many special thanks to Jo Kyle who has done such a magnificent job with the editing of these books. Working with Jo in cyberspace has opened my eyes up to the amazing potential of electronic relationships. I have learned to trust and respect the judgement of someone simply through the exchange of written words. (A good lesson for a writer!)

Thirdly the Thorsons team have been as patient, supportive and willing to experiment as ever. A big thank you to each and every one of you.

Finally, once again my husband Stuart's contribution must be acknowledged. The title of this series was his idea. As ever, I am also grateful to him for his giving over so much of his precious free time to editing my dyslexic manuscripts before they leave the privacy of our home.

Contents

Stage 1: Develop the Attributes of a Decisive Person

Stage 2: Prepare Yourself for Action!

Introduction to the
Shortcuts Series

At this moment in your life, reading a book is probably one of the last things you feel like doing. If so, you are exactly the kind of reader I had in mind when I designed this Shortcuts series!

I have struggled with enough personal problems myself to know that when you are in the throes of them, the thought of wading through any book is daunting. You just haven't got the concentration or the motivation. When I am in this situation, all I long for is for someone to tell me what to do – or, even better, relieve me of my hurt or worry by taking it away from me!

So I would like you to think of these Shortcuts guides not so much as books, but as supportive tools. I do not intend them to be an absorbing 'read' to take to the sofa or bath and get 'lost' in. On the contrary, they are designed as 'ready-made' strategies to help kick you into action – and to keep you moving over a period of one or two months – at least! (Isn't 'the getting going' always the hardest part of solving any problem? This is when I have found that even the most competent and self-reliant people can benefit from support.)

But it is also important that when we do get started, we begin in a *constructive* way. A common mistake is to *do* the first thing that comes into our mind. This can make us feel better because we feel more in control. But this 'hit and miss' approach often gets us going on a very much longer and rockier road than we need have taken. In contrast, these Shortcut strategies will guide you along a route that has been meticulously planned. They are derived from years of experimentation and studying other people's tried and tested paths.

The first characteristic of each book that you may notice (and perhaps find initially frustrating) is that they all start with some preparation work. This is because, in my experience, diving headlong into the heart of the problem often proves to be the short-cut to failure!

After you have prepared yourself, the strategy moves along in a series of small steps, each with its own section. Although sometimes these steps will overlap, most of the time you should find that one naturally follows on from the other. At the end of each, you will find a list of tips called 'Action time!' Some of the suggestions and exercises contained in this section may work better for you than others. But I am confident that in the process of trying them, you are much more likely to find out what will help than if you did nothing at all! So I hope you will find them of use one way or another.

Throughout the book you will also find some quotes and key 'messages'. I hope you will find these useful should you just want to dip into the book and gain some quick support and guidance at times when the going feels tough.

Finally, I would like you to always bear in mind that in the personal development field there are no prizes for being first to the winning post. But there are, however, plenty of rewards to be had from the *effective* learning of problem-solving skills. So if you proceed through these Shortcuts books at a pace which feels **comfortably challenging,** you will have learned an invaluable skill that could save you time and energy for the rest of your life.

Enjoy the journey! (Yes, problem-solving *can* be highly pleasurable!)

The strongest principle of human growth lies in human choice.

GEORGE ELIOT

Introduction

The more choice we have, the freer we are.

That's the theory – but is that your experience?

Mankind, we are often told, has never had it so good. For the first time in our history we have the whole world (not to mention some other parts of the universe) within our reach. We have never had so many options and so many opportunities. No generation has ever been so 'spoilt for choice' and never been so free to choose.

A party of visitors from just one century ago might expect to find us all jumping with joy and gratitude. Instead, they would probably be shocked to see so many tortured faces staring powerlessly up from their unhappy ruts. They would find it hard to believe that such an abundance of choice could have given birth to this disabling new plague called 'Indecisiveness'!

I belong to one of the many new professions which has now evolved to help cure this modern malaise. Much of my career has been devoted to helping people choose whether or not to:

- walk out on partners who they know are no good for them
- sign up for long costly courses that promise to fulfil their potential
- stop renting flats/houses and tie themselves to a mortgage
- leave well-paid but boring or stressful jobs
- bring more children into a dangerous world
- stay at home with the baby or return to work
- move 5,000 miles away from ageing parents
- stick up for their own rights in the face of others' hurt or anger
- allow their teens to travel the world without them
- implement policies at work they know to be unfair
- take drugs that claim to make them happy or calm
- and so on ...

Like so many of these people, I also reached adulthood totally unprepared for the responsibility of choosing the kind of life I wanted, or what kind of person I wanted to become, or how I wanted to behave. Like them, I found the sheer quantity of options before me quite terrifying. I had even lost faith in the religion which used to direct and console me.

So, I had to learn how to choose the hard way – by making many appalling mistakes. Some of these I don't regret – I am wiser for them. But the vast majority were an avoidable waste of my life. And, moreover, they often hurt and hindered others as well.

So if you are currently confronting a hard choice and feel ill-equipped to make your decision, you are right to be anxious. You are also right to seek guidance. But I am well aware that not everyone wants to (or can afford to!) pour their indecisiveness into the lap of therapists like me. That's why I decided to write this book. I hope it will provide you with a practical self-help tool that you can use over and over again to help you make difficult decisions. However, I also hope that one day you will reach the point when you can throw it away!

Fast, efficient decision-making *is* an easy-to-learn skill which, with practice, can become a life-transforming habit!

What is the
Shortcut Strategy?

As you will see, our Shortcut strategy for making hard choices easy is divided into five stages:

STAGE 1: Develop the Attributes of a Decisive Person

STAGE 2: Prepare Yourself for Action!

STAGE 3: Expand and Contract Your Options

STAGE 4: Make Your Final Choice

STAGE 5: Stick by Your Choice with Confidence

As I mentioned earlier, within each of these stages there are a number of different steps to work through. It is important to work through these steps in the order I have suggested, and it is also important not to skip any. Inevitably, sometimes there may be some overlap, but generally speaking each step should follow on quite naturally from the previous one.

The five stages

The first two stages in our strategy are the preparation stages. In **Stage 1** we will look at some ways you can develop aspects of your personality which will strengthen your overall decision-making ability. Then in **Stage 2** we will explore some ways you can prepare your body and mind so that you will be in the best possible shape for the task ahead.

By the time you reach **Stage 3**, you will be fully prepared for the core part of the decision-making process. In this stage we will look at the best ways to search for and then analyse the information on the subject relating to your choice.

In **Stage 4** we will work through some tried and tested methods for making difficult decisions, and we will look at *how* to make your final decision. And then, finally, in **Stage 5** we will look at some steps you can take to help you move on and ensure that your choice has the best chance of being successful.

Please remember that you must proceed through the stages at your own pace. My guess is that for most people a couple of hours a week over one or two months will prove to be the right pace for working through this strategy.

Even though life has a habit of coming up with unexpected surprises and extra commitments, it is important to make some kind of outline timetable (for example, note down at least an anticipated time for completing each step) and then clear spaces in your diary to do the exercises. This will help to keep you motivated as well as ensuring that you actually have enough time available.

I hope you will find that working through this strategy will be interesting and enlightening, as well as helping you to make your hard choice much more easily.

Stage One

develop the attributes of a decisive person

People who *consistently* make hard choices with more ease than others commonly share certain key personality attributes. In this stage you will learn what these are and how you can develop them.

I appreciate that your concern right now is probably focused almost entirely on the one decision you are currently trying to make. So doing this general personality work may seem like an irritating digression. But I hope you will stick with it. Not only will it help you to make your choice more quickly when you do return to looking at it, but it will also help you become more decisive in your everyday life. Just think of how much time, energy and possibly money this could save you! And to add to these bonuses, you will probably earn extra respect from yourself and others. Dithering is not a personal quality that has a reputation for increasing esteem.

So why not put your choice aside for a short while and refocus your energy on becoming a decisive person both now and forever!

STEP 1

Build your self-confidence and resilience

Lack of self-confidence and fear are the two biggest saboteurs of decision-making.

If a choice is hard it is usually because there is at least one risk involved. The risk could be that you may lose money, a job, a person you love, an opportunity or esteem. Alternatively, you could be worried that you might hurt yourself or others, or the outcome of your choice might not be as enjoyable or beneficial as you thought it would be.

Decisive people can take the heat of living with risk. This is because their **self-confidence** helps them to believe that firstly, they *are* capable of making good choices, and secondly, it reassures them that if they do end up making the wrong decision they can, and will, cope with the consequences. They have a deep inner trust in their capabilities and their survivability.

Courage is also a key characteristic of decisive people and it plays its part by helping them to keep control of their fears. (And yes, they are often just as frightened as anyone else!)

Are you as confident and courageous as you can be? Probably not – because who is?!

Most of us can do with a boost of both confidence and courage before we make a hard choice. But some of us may need it more than others. For example, those of you who are timid by nature or those of you who are still feeling bruised by the effects of some past bad choices will, understandably, be more frightened than others.

Similarly, those of you whose self-esteem is generally low and shaky (for whatever reason) will also be finding it harder than most to make your choice. I am sure you don't need me to tell you that, more often than not, when faced with a decision you automatically think you will choose badly. Right now you are probably fearing the worst and worrying about what others will think when you get it wrong!

Here is something more constructive that you can do instead!

Giving your courage and confidence a boost before making a hard choice will shorten your decision-making time.

**Worry is the greatest enemy
of a good decision.
Worry, it has been said, is like a
rocking chair. It will keep you moving
but it doesn't get you anywhere.**

LOU ANN SMITH, *BE DECISIVE*

Action time!

- **Start acting in a more self-loving way.** Treat treats as essentials and start giving yourself at least one or two small ones every day. (For example, however stressed or busy I am I always make time to have regular leisurely breaks with fresh coffee or jasmine tea and a book or magazine that I don't need to read.) But be even more generous to yourself whenever you are feeling disappointed, hurt or anxious. Until treat-giving becomes a well-entrenched habit, keep a check on yourself by inserting a small symbolic mark in your diary or calendar each day.

- **Follow the lead of successful athletes and sports stars and use encouraging self-talk to motivate yourself.** Feeding your mind regularly with statements such as 'I can do it', 'I can be decisive' and 'I am courageous' undoubtedly works. (And, of course, negative self-talk is equally effective if you want to de-motivate yourself!)

- **Use your imagination to plant positive mental 'movies' in your brain.** Use your own favourite technique to get your body into a deeply-relaxed state (see the following box for a suggestion) and then visualize yourself being super-confident in situations where you normally feel timid (for example, speaking your mind in meetings or initiating conversations with strangers at parties). Play the scene in your mind as though you were viewing it on a giant cinema screen with full colour and clear digital sound. Notice and take pleasure in the sense of power the vision brings. The more you blast your senses with the image and feel the accompanying emotion, the better this technique will work. Repeat several times just before going into the situation in real-life.

A Quick and Easy Relaxation Technique

1. Firstly, give your muscles a good stretch, focusing particularly on the ones you know hold most tension in your body. (As I spend a lot of time working at a computer, for me this is my shoulder and neck muscles.)
2. Next, do a minute of marching on the spot, gradually increasing your pace but not to the

point of exhaustion. (Yes, like the soldiers! Left arm and right knee up and then right arm and left knee.)

3. Now take some slow deep breaths, while concentrating hard on the flow of your breath in and out of your body.

4. Next, stand or sit in a comfortable well-supported position. Place the fingertips of your hands together and hold them in an easy relaxed position pointing downwards.

5. Finally, close your eyes and repeat this phrase slowly five times: 'I am cool, calm and in control.'

- **Do one dare a day**. Start by making a minor change in your lifestyle or habits. Your new challenges should give you a *manageable* degree of anxiety (i.e. they should be those you can do without having to reach for the bottle or depend on someone else to push you 'off the ledge'!). Gradually increase the difficulty of your dares, and don't forget to reward yourself with a treat after each. (For example, day one – try taking lunch or having a drink on your own somewhere you have never tried before; day five – strike up a conversation with someone in a café or bar.)

- **Forgive yourself for past bad decisions.** Don't let your self-esteem be eroded by guilt and regret. Write down on a card three examples of bad decisions you have made in the past and the lessons you learned from them. (For example, taking out that extra loan – taught me how easy it is for me to slip into unmanageable debt; moving in with John – taught me how much personal space I need and how important living in an uncluttered place is to me!) Read these examples (or bring them to mind) whenever you or anyone else pushes your regret or guilt buttons.

- **Buy a self-help book on fear management or confidence-building, such as Susan Jeffers's** *Feel the Fear and Do It Anyway* **or my book** *Super Confidence*. (See the *Further help* section at the end of the book for details.)

- **Play a tape on fear management or confidence-building on your way to work or while you are doing your routine chores.** If the tape does not use rousing music, follow it by listening to some inspirational music of your own choice.

STEP 2

Focus the direction of your life

Decisive people don't dither. No time or energy is wasted hanging around the cross-roads of their lives. Why not?

The secret is simple – preparatory homework! Long before they reach a crunch decision-making point in their journey through life, they have:

- developed a clear vision of their desired destination. (For example, who they want to be, what they want to be doing, and so forth.)
- studied the map and have planned the best route for them. They have already made up their mind about the quality of the journey they want, so they do not dither over whether they should take the scenic route or the motorway. (For example, whether they want a

laid-back peaceful lifestyle or a fast competitive one.)
- **taken into consideration the price they are prepared to pay.** So, should they meet 'tolls' on their journey, they don't waste time worrying about whether to pay them or turn around. They know the value of their destination and what the journey holds for them. (For example, whether the mortgage rate or demanding boss are worth the expense and hassle.)

Of course, the unforeseen may still happen to decisive people as it can to anyone. Through no fault of their own, they can find a tractor blocking their way (for example, an unexpectedly difficult exam); have a blow-out in the fast lane (for example, an illness); find fuel prices are escalating (for example, interest rates are soaring), or meet a friend who tells them their dream destination is being cut-off (for example, their employer is going bust). But, unlike indecisive people, when this happens they don't waste time berating themselves or fate for their bad luck. Instead, they 'go back to the drawing board' and re-review their life-plan and their values.

Are you as clear as you can be about the kind of life you want to lead and what you want to achieve? Do you know what kind of price you are prepared to pay in order to get what you really want?

If you are persistently unable to make difficult choices, then it is unlikely that you can answer either of these questions very readily. Perhaps you haven't even realized this truth before. Many people don't until they are confronted with a particularly difficult life choice. It is only then that they realize that they have slipped into a rut of other people's choosing. This is because most of the influences operate at a subconscious level. Unless we have been encouraged to question and confront our 'operating' values and principles, we may not even know which ones are driving us. Even if we do, we may think, quite wrongly, that they are our own.

Whether we like it or not, we are conditioned creatures. The majority of our beliefs, habits, aspirations and values are shaped by our 'inheritance' – our religion, the culture of our country and influential parent-figures – long before we know the meaning of the words 'value' and 'goal'. (We will be discussing our 'inheritance' further in Step 8.)

Even when we have become an adult, the 'programming' process continues. Each day we are prey to a multitude of subconscious forces which mould our personality without our conscious consent. These can come in the shape of role-modelling from, for example, a workaholic parent or apathetic colleagues; motivational 'carrots' such as share options or medals, or seductive adverts offering mega-discounts and propaganda promising national glory. But they can come even more subtly as emotional 'hooks' from the people we love. You would be very unusual if you had never felt the 'pull' of pleasing your parents, partner or friends.

As these influences on our beliefs and values come from so many sources there is very little co-ordination between them. So we may find ourselves unconsciously pulled in one direction by our father's ambitious streak, but in another by the example given by our laid-back friends or colleagues. Or we may find ourselves pulled both by our old school's motto to 'Do as you would be done by' and our company's 'dog-eat-dog' culture.

If you want to be a decisive person, *you* must assume control over such forces. You must be firmly rooted in the driving seat of your own life. Taking the time and trouble to clarify your *own* guiding principles, and developing a crystal-clear vision of the future that *you* want, is the only way you can do this. Here are some exercises that will help you to do this more speedily.

> **Clarifying your dreams, goals and values will put you firmly in the driving seat of your own life.**

**If you don't know where
you are going,
you will probably end
up somewhere else.**

DR LAURENCE PETER

Action time!

You will need some paper and a pen or pencil for the following exercises.

- **Complete each of the following sentences with six answers:**

  By the time I reach retirement age I must have ...
  In 20 years' time I would like to be ...
  On a perfect day for me you would see me ...
  The qualities in people whom I admire most are ...
  I feel ashamed when I ...
  I am most proud of myself when I am being ...
  The things that give me most stress in life are ...
  My greatest regrets are ...
  If I was told that I had a very limited time to live I would make sure that I ...

- **Cross out three answers for each sentence you have completed, leaving the ones which are most important to you.** (Yes, more hard choices, but worth it because it will help you to clarify your values!)

- **Write a subtitle for a biography you would like someone to write on you after your death.** (One that concisely sums up the essence of how you would like to be remembered!) For example, the subtitle of Tanya Stone's biography on Diana, Princess of Wales sums up the essence of her – *Princess of the People* (Millbrook Press, 1997), as does the subtitle of Vincent Hardy's biography on Martin Luther King – *The Inconvenient Hero* (Orbis, 1996).

- **List the six most important values or principles which ideally you would like to be guiding your life.** (For example, integrity / independence / security / compassion / adventure / peace of mind / fun / intimacy / and so forth.) Write these on a small card, and carry the card around with you for the next few weeks and read the list often. Each time you face a difficult choice, however small (such as, should I spend 10% more on organic tomatoes or not!), think of your values list before you make that choice.

STEP 3

Rebalance your thinking powers

Hard choices are usually *important* choices. They deserve the very best of our thinking potential. Most of us rarely use this. We don't need to. The pace of modern life demands speedy perception and thinking. This means that our brains are, more often than not, working in 'auto-response mode'. This is fine for our everyday choices, such as when a friend rings and asks us if we'd like to meet for a drink today or tomorrow. They only demand a quick 'good-enough' pre-programmed reaction. But we are definitely short-changing ourselves if we do not access the full range of our conscious thinking powers when we are faced with a more major decision, for example, another friend ringing to ask us to take a year off to go on a trip around the world.

When we are operating in auto-mode we are usually using our dominant thinking traits more than our less developed ones. For example, I have been pro-grammed by nature (and probably by nurture) as a female to use my right brain more than my left brain for thinking. This means that I am more 'automati-cally inclined' towards functioning intuitively rather than analytically. Therefore, when I am faced with everyday decisions, I often go with the choice that 'feels' right rather than get into the kind of speedy calculations that my left-brained husband would use. Apart from causing the odd minor marital tiff, my 'natural' thinking approach works well-enough for most minor choices. For example, when I am choosing who to chat to at a conference or which restaurant to try out next, the risks are minimal. (As an introvert I don't need that many friends, and I always have a stock of bananas to fill the gaps left by inferior meals!)

However, should I use my 'gut' rather than my 'head' to make more serious choices, I know that it can let me down very badly. I have many embarrass-ing memories of 'silly' emotional decisions in my past love-life and early career. These serve as a great reminder that before making a serious choice

I must consciously depress my instinctive reaction while I consult my more 'sensible' left brain.

Through my work I have also known many people with the opposite experience. They have made many bad choices because they have been inclined towards taking a hard-headed left-brain approach to decision-making.

> **Most hard choices need and deserve the conscious attention of our *whole* brain.**

You too were born with a preference for using certain centres of your brain more than others. You will also have had life experiences which have developed some thinking centres more than others.

Are you aware of your brain's strengths and weaknesses? Are you sure that you have developed enough of your decision-making potential?

Remember that we are often most prejudiced and biased when looking at ourselves! So it could be helpful to ask for some feedback from others who you can depend on to give you a straight, honest answer. You could show them the following exercise and ask them to rate you on each of these important thinking qualities.

To gain maximum happiness and fufilment you require a repertoire of thinking skills. You are personally responsible for your thinking choices and for developing and using appropriate thinking skills when faced with personal problems. Effective and independent thinking can require courage.

RICHARD NELSON-JONES,
EFFECTIVE THINKING SKILLS

Action time!

Examine the following list of thinking qualities needed to be a good decision-maker. Rate yourself in terms of strengths and weaknesses. If you get a score lower than three, note down what you are going to do to increase your thinking power in that area.

1. **Intuitive** – you know what feels right or wrong, even if you do not act on it

[weak 1 _____ 6 strong]

Low scorers could, for example, practise 'going with their first instinctive reaction' when making low-risk everyday decisions and talk through their choices with more intuitive people.

2. **Analytical** – you calculate the odds meticulously and objectively

[weak 1 _____ 6 strong]

Low scorers could use their calculator and computer more to help them or they could join a maths class. They should take particular note of Stage 4 of this book.

3. **Ordered** – you make action plans, strategies and lists

[weak 1 _____ 6 strong]

Low scorers could make a daily prioritized 'To Do' list and practise assertively saying 'No' to anything not on this list. They could also take particular note of the latter stages of this book.

4. **Logical** – you work systematically through a process and do not jump randomly from one idea to the next

[weak 1 _____ 6 strong]

Low scorers could ask friends to let them know when their mind is 'jumping' (they rarely know themselves), or sign up for an evening course in basic philosophy which teaches logic.

5. **Sensitive** – you are fully aware of your emotions and take into account the influence and information from all of your senses. You are also good at sensing the emotional states of others

[weak 1 _____ 6 strong]

Low scorers could make a habit of stopping frequently to listen to their bodies (we sense our emotions physically before we are aware of them in our mind) and buy or borrow a book on body language.

6. **Creative** – you are able to come up with new ideas and approaches

[weak 1 _____ 6 strong]

Low scorers could spend more time with young children and energize their spontaneity and playfulness. They could also ask for 'wild and wacky' ideas and alternative options from creative people before making their choices. They should take particular note of Stage 3 of this book.

Stage Two

prepare yourself for action!

In this stage you will be creating a space in your life to give your choice the due consideration it deserves. You will also be preparing your body and mind so that they are both in the best possible shape for the hard decision-making you have to do. So keep your choice firmly on the backburner for a little while longer. Remember, you are not procrastinating, you are preparing. So if you start to fret about the time you are taking on this stage, just remind yourself how much longer most jobs take to do if the ground and tools you need for them are not ready or in good shape. Picture yourself trying to cook a good meal in an over-heated kitchen where surfaces are cluttered and knives are blunt!

**Not deciding is deciding
But ... deciding to wait is OK**

LOU ANN SMITH

STEP 4

Allow yourself some quality thinking time

A sure-fire way to sabotage your chances of making a good choice is simply not to give yourself enough quality time to think. However obvious this truth may sound it is one that I constantly find is forgotten in real life. Even though someone may be fully aware of how many hours they are wasting worrying about the fact that they haven't made their decision, I still have a hard job convincing most people that they need to set aside a period of time to do nothing but think.

So, once again, I make no apologies for reminding you about the obvious!

To choose time is to save time.

FRANCIS BACON

> **If you don't give your conscious mind some constructive thinking time, your unconscious mind will ensure that you worry until you reach a point of desperation.**

Perhaps in the past you have found yourself forced into a corner by your mind like this – and you have lived to regret it. Maybe you have worried yourself 'sick' and then, when you 'couldn't take it any more', found yourself no longer caring what you did or what happened!

Unless we are very lucky, when we allow ourselves to reach such a point we *often* make bad decisions. This is because when we are stressed or depressed our brain's capacity to think constructively is seriously impaired.

Alternatively, in this state we may be only too willing to let others do our choosing for us. I have known many people jog along in a state of dissatisfaction in a job because they do not allow themselves time to look at the alternatives and plan

Procrastination is the thief of time.

EDWARD YOUNG

for the consequences of making the choice to leave. The employer, noticing their lack of motivation, then makes the decision for them and they are left with a serious black mark on their CV.

Many personal relationships also end in a similarly unsatisfactory way. Both partners may be unhappy, not because they lack love and respect for each other, but because their contrasting needs makes living together too difficult. The result is that they either store up resentment or openly bicker until one of them reaches their breaking point. With hindsight, they can see that if only they had given themselves some quality time to seriously think through their options, they could probably have parted without a destructive crisis.

I am convinced that the success of much therapy and counselling is to do with the fact that it provides people with this kind of 'enforced' quality thinking time. My clients often try to give me the credit when they reach the point when their choice 'magically' becomes easy. But the truth often is that, by setting them homework tasks, all I have done is given them 'permission' – or a gentle push! – to set aside periods of time to carefully consider their choice.

Are you sabotaging yourself with poor thinking-time management? One test you could give yourself would be to look right now at whether you are allowing yourself *quality* time to read this book.

Hard choices need QUALITY thinking time which is:

- set aside solely for the purpose of helping you with your choice
- taken in a peaceful environment (which allows you to concentrate without distraction)
- not interrupted by the needs of others
- long enough to allow you to think seriously (for example, 20 minutes minimum and *not* a snatched 5 minutes here and there)
- worry-free (because your mind is otherwise engaged in constructive problem solving activity)

Those who make the worst use of time are those who complain of its brevity.

JEAN DE LA BRUYÈRE

Action time!

- **Make a list of the ten most urgent tasks you must complete during the next two weeks.** Now rate your tasks in order of priority.

- **In consultation with your diary, and bearing in mind the priority rating you gave each task, put an allocated period of time beside each task** (i.e. the total number of hours or minutes you will need to spend on each).

- **Using a coloured highlighter pen, mark some of the free periods which are left over in your diary as quality thinking time.** These should be at least half an hour in length and you will probably need at least four, but preferably six of these (i.e. a total of two to three hours) to do the work you need to do to ensure you make a good choice. If you appear to have no free time available, review the allocations of time you gave to each of your tasks. Reduce these wherever you can. (Remember that unless you do, you will risk making a bad choice or no choice at all!)

If you are at work and you think people will think you are too freely available if you enter 'thinking time' into your diary, you could consider using a white lie or two! A secret trick of many successful business people I know is to give a name to a non-existent project. They then enter appointments for this project into their diary to protect periods of time which they need for thinking.

- **Make a copy of your schedule and give it to a trusted friend who may be able to help you protect this time.** This is another good trick for people whose time is highly pressurized and are too often at other people's beck and call. (Have you ever been told 'She's in a meeting' when you know she is there?!)

STEP 5

Flex your decision-making muscles

If you were struggling with the last exercise simply because you couldn't find space in your diary, the following exercises should help. By giving yourself lots of practice in the art of everyday decision-making, as well as trying to make choices faster, you will save a surprising amount of time which you can then devote more constructively to your major life choices.

Because nowadays even our everyday options tend to be so numerous, most of us are spending far longer than we need to on decisions that are of little consequence. Let's look at the choices we have when performing some very mundane tasks:

- **travel to our local shopping centre:** once upon a time we would have had no choice but to use our legs to walk us there. Now we may have to decide whether we should take the bus, the car, a taxi, a train or the tram, or get a bike or scooter out of the shed. How many hours are wasted in arguments with ourselves and our families about the best way of getting from A to B?

- **tonight's meal**: once we would have had to eat whatever we had been able to kill or whatever our garden had grown for us. There may have been only one pot to cook it in. Now we often have three giant supermarkets on our doorstep, plus many other sources of food from all over the world, and shelves of recipe books to choose from.
- **choosing books or magazines to take on holiday**: once there was no choice. Now those of us living in large towns have not only three or four large stores to buy books from, but also libraries and the internet to search through before selecting the 'perfect' holiday companions. (And how many of these return unopened because we found more appealing things to do?!)

I don't want to belittle these kinds of everyday choices. They can, after all, have a very positive impact on our quality of life. I am just suggesting that you think about the times that you make life more difficult for yourself by agonising unnecessarily over these choices. For example, the next time you spend an exhausting afternoon shopping, only to return to buy the first item you saw, think about the treats you could have given yourself during that same time, or that outstanding job you could have cleared from your 'To Do' list.

Or, the next time you dilly-dally over whether or not to strike up a conversation with an interesting-looking stranger, remind yourself that few people's conversation is as boring as the 'Should I or shouldn't I?' conversation that is inhabiting your head.

'Petty' indecisiveness can waste life's great opportunities!

**The way to make better decisions
is to make more of them ...
repetition is the mother of skill.
Good judgement is the result of
experience.**

ANTHONY ROBBINS, *AWAKEN THE GIANT WITHIN*

Action time!

- **Take four sheets of paper. At the top of each page write one of the following headings:**

  1. Nickel
  2. Bronze
  3. Silver
  4. Gold

  Over the next few days note down as many choices you can think of that you have to make in your life and enter them onto one of the pages as appropriate. Each of us must decide for ourselves what 'weight' of importance we give our individual choices, but the following might be a useful guide.

  Gold choices – these are your *strategic / policy* ones. They are the major choices that shape the direction of your life on its path towards your ultimate long-term goals. They might include your choice of:

  > life partner; whether or not to have children; job; career or important hobby

training programmes; location to live in; style and price of accommodation; political allegiance or change of religion; schools for children, and so forth.

Silver choices – these are your day-to-day *life management* ones. They are important choices with considerable risk sometimes involved. But they are not the most important ones you will ever make. They might include your choice of:

staff at work; projects you undertake; decor for your accommodation or office; major expenses on cars, holidays, hobbies and raising children, and so forth.

Bronze choices – these are your *everyday* ones. Individually they may not seem very important but because they are repeated often they will affect the overall quality and balance of your life. They can be the biggest time-wasters of all our choices. They might include your choice of:

how to travel; overall diet; clothes to buy and when to wear what; which tasks to put on your daily 'To Do' list; which lawn mower or vacuum cleaner is best, and so forth.

Nickel choices – these are the really *inconsequential* decisions. This is the area you can use for your initial practice. They might include your choice of:

newspapers or magazines; TV programmes; motorway stops; routes to take; filing systems; snacks; wines or beers, and so forth.

- **Beside each example, note down the amount of time which, in the light of your values** (see Step 2) **and your life situation, would be reasonable to take over this choice.**

- **Over the next week or so, whenever you are faced with a choice, however small, consider in which category it belongs.** Pay special attention to the nickel and bronze ones and ensure that they do not take up any more time than you have allocated to them.

- **Reward yourself with a treat in the time you have saved.** (Workaholics – don't worry, you won't have to use your saved minutes this way for ever. Remember, once the new decision-making habit is established, the time is yours for keeps!)

Take an energizing break

Making a hard choice is *always* stressful. Inevitably, the process of researching the options, dealing with the fear of risk and the hard thinking puts extra pressure on both our bodies and our minds. In an ideal world we would only make these kinds of decisions when we were at our peak of physical fitness and mental agility. But, of course, the reality is that they often confront us just when we are scraping the barrel of our energy reserves!

Sometimes it is exhaustion itself which forces us to face the difficult choice. I know that several times in my life I have only seriously considered leaving an unsatisfactory job or relationship when I reached the point when I 'could take no more'.

The dangers of doing your thinking in such a state are probably obvious. But I make no apologies for reminding you about them! This is because I guess that right now, like most people who are worrying about a hard choice, taking time-out to rest won't figure high on your list of priorities. So here is your reminder!

When we are in a state of high stress our nervous system switches into emergency mode. (This is commonly known as the fight/flight/freeze response.) Depending on your personality and also the kind of threat you perceive yourself to be up against, you are likely to be feeling frustrated and angry, or frightened and powerless. Your heart will be working overtime and your body will have stiffened with tension. Also, very importantly, because your brain thinks an urgent response is called for, it will have dampened down its more sophisticated thinking centres and be searching through its more primitive archives for an immediate 'blue-print' solution rather than a well-thought-through or new approach. (This is why you may now be haunted by your embarrassingly simplistic approach to some quick decisions you have made in the past.)

I assume that, as you are taking the time to read this book, your current hard choice does not come into the category of one of life's emergencies that needs attention NOW! So I am trusting that you do have the time now to calm your nervous system down and reclaim the full potential of your human (rather than animal!) brain.

By taking time out to relax you will reclaim the full power of your decision-making potential.

It is time to move away from the problem when the same solution keeps recurring but doesn't seem the perfect answer. Physically removing yourself from the decision-making arena reduces your anxiety level. At the very centre of inner calm is mental clarity.

ROGER DAWSON,
THE CONFIDENT DECISION MAKER

Action time!

- **Fill your fridge and store cupboard with high-quality mind and body energizing foods.**

- **Cut down on your intake of alcohol at least a week before starting your thinking.** (I assume your choice is important-enough to deserve your full faculties!)

- **Scan your diary – choose a free period of at least two hours** (the harder your choice, the longer you need). If you have done the exercises in Steps 4 and 5 you should have made some quality time available. Mark this as protected time for a relaxation and motivation session.

- **Decide where you will go for your relaxation session – the further it is from the decision-making environment the better.** (You could try and convince your nearest and dearest that a beach in Fiji may be ideal, but I'm afraid the truth is that a quiet, locked room at home or work would suffice!)

- **If you are physically very tense, for the first hour of your session you could book a relaxation session with a professional** (for example, an aromatherapist, a massage therapist or a stress consultant). Alternatively, do your own favourite self-help relaxation (see page 17 for a quick and easy relaxation technique). Whatever method you use, just remember that your aim is to get yourself into the physiological state where your pulse is considerably slower than usual, your limbs feel loose and floppy, and your mind is floating rather than thinking or worrying. You should be able to do this *without* falling asleep. If you can't, then wait until you have had some early nights and try again.

- **When you have finished your relaxation, use the second hour to put yourself in a good mood**. Give yourself a treat and do an activity which you can guarantee will be enjoyable for you. (This is not the time for experimenting with new avenues for fun so stick to your favourites!)

- **Finish by writing down on a sticky note the positive emotions you *will* feel when you have finally removed your choice from off your back.** (For example: *'When I have made my choice I will feel relief / freedom / ecstatic / more confident',* and so forth.)

- **Close your eyes and picture yourself feeling those feelings.** Consciously intensify the feelings for a few minutes and notice the effect that they are having on your body. For the next few days, just before going to bed (perhaps when you are preparing your night-cap), take a minute to close your eyes and feel these good feelings once again.

- **To help maintain this energized and optimistic state, place the sticky note where your unconscious mind can glance at it frequently** (for example, the kitchen cupboard, your computer or the back of the loo door).

Stage Three

expand and contract your options

Preparation time is now over. At last you have reached the 'meaty' business in the decision-making process. In this stage you will be doing exercises which will help you first to gather the information you need; then you will expand your options and look at them with a critical eye, and finally you will be reducing these options until you are left with only two from which to choose.

If you are thinking that you already have only two options, please do still work through the first few steps of this stage. You may well find after having done the exercises that there are more options available to you than you thought. Contrary to what you think, finding more options will not make the decision-process even longer. It often reduces it. When we feel cornered by having too few options we tend to feel more powerless and therefore are less confident and capable. And anyway, don't forget that perhaps one of the reasons why you are finding your choice so hard could be that neither of the options you currently think you have is the right one for you!

STEP 7

Saturate yourself with information

Now you are going to search out information from as many sources as you can which could throw some light on the issues surrounding your choice.

I love this stage. Choosing what to put and what not to put in a book is for me the toughest and most stressful aspect of being a writer. So I love being able to give myself full permission to put my choices on the backburner while I freely indulge myself with enlightenment from others! The problem is that I often find it difficult to move on from this research stage. The 'high' that I experience when I am in this 'discovery' mode warps my ability to know when enough is enough! I can always find a reason why I must have more information before moving on.

This is a problem that I have found many indecisive people share. Quite often by the time they consult me they have already overdosed on research and advice from others. They feel desperate for a 'kick' to move them out from under the mountain of information they have acquired. Although a small sadistic part of me would love to oblige, I often have to do the opposite! Because the quality of the research they have already done is so bad, I have to suggest they return to square one. This isn't because they are unintelligent or slapdash, it is because while they were gathering their information they were operating in the kind of negative panic state which I discussed in Step 6.

But don't worry, there is no danger of this happening to you. After all, you have (haven't you?!) dutifully taken time-out to de-stress and you are now fully able to take an organized and realistically timed approach to your research. Because you are also in an optimistic mood, you are bound to find the good rather than bad news. You will review apparently depressing statistics and doom-laden advice from sceptics with calm objectivity.

I hope you enjoy your research as much as I do. But I also hope that you will be better behaved than I am at sticking to the deadline you give yourself for its completion!

> **Two hours of information-seeking done in a positive mood can be more valuable than a week's worth of research done with a bad attitude!**

The tough decisions are not necessarily the big ones. For example, prioritising the order in which you do things – weighing up the different merits of competing and apparently equally important demands on limited resources – can be very tough. Emotion and sentiment can be difficult walls. Accurate information is the key currency and you can't have enough.

MARK BYFORD, DIRECTOR,
BBC WORLD SERVICE

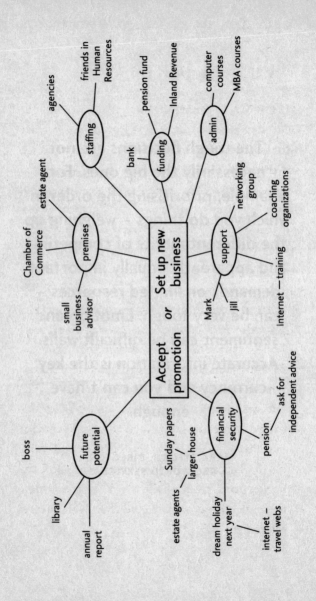

Action time!

IMPORTANT REMINDER! *When doing the following exercises, at this stage you want* **only information** *on the subject matter of your dilemma,* **not direct advice** *from others about what decision you should make. Some people might need to be told (gently or not-so-gently!) that this is* **your** *choice and* **you** *are going to make it when, and only when, you have fully researched your options.*

- **Brainstorm your potential sources of information and help – for example, certain friends and colleagues, organizations, books, internet sites, agencies, and so forth.** (See the illustration opposite.) Show your brainstorm to several knowledgeable and wise friends or colleagues and ask them to add suggestions. Make a list of people who may be affected by your choice and take particular care to include, whenever you can, suggestions from them. (It is a good idea to mark these with a red pen for future reference.)

- **Sort the information and suggestions into approximately six categories.** (Many more and you will begin to feel overwhelmed.) Each category can contain subdivisions if you think these might be useful. You can make up your own or use the ones I have listed below:

Statistics and facts
- costs which may be incurred through putting your choice into action
- number of people who could be affected by your decision
- what the risks are
- what the law is

Theoretical information
- relevant books
- relevant articles
- useful internet sites

Life-experience material
- own past experiences
- autobiographies of people who have made the choice
- relevant films/documentaries

The optimists
- positive friends
- people you know who made a good choice in the same area and have experience to share
- supportive colleagues
- professionals with a positive viewpoint

The challengers
- the experiences of people who have made a bad choice in the same area
- confrontative colleagues and friends – those who have contrasting approaches to this kind of situation
- professionals who have different or specialist knowledge

The creative minds
- people you know who are innovative (for example, entrepreneurs and artists)
- radical thinkers you'd like to contact or read (for example, cutting-edge theorists and consultants)

- **Make a folder for each category.** You can do this on a computer but, unless you have a scanner, you may prefer the old-fashioned card type of folder. You need to be able easily to insert bits and pieces (such as articles and clippings) into it as you find them, so you can deal with them when you have time.

- **Set a deadline date for filling these folders.** This date should be 'challenging' enough to keep you on your toes with the task, but also give you a realistic chance to gather the information. So have a good look at the next month or two of commitments in your diary before setting it.

Time pressure can, in fact, be helpful – it concentrates the mind, rules out procrastination, and reduces the number of alternatives that can be considered.

ROBERT HELLER, *MAKING DECISIONS*

STEP 8

Challenge your 'inheritance'

You have already considered some aspects of the 'inheritance' you have lodged in your subconscious mind when you were examining your values and attitudes in Step 2. Now we will look at its influence in relation to the choice with which you are now faced.

Every choice we make will be influenced to *some* degree by the information that has previously been loaded into the thinking and emotional memory centres in our brain. This will colour our attitude, perception and emotional response. It is as though we are looking at our choice through a screen – a very unique screen fabricated from a web made from strands of our own unique experiences and genetic make-up. Let's look at an example:

If I, as an employer, am faced with a hard choice about whether or not to make an older senior employee redundant, whether I like it or not my brain will immediately start doing its own research amongst its archives. It will scan my memory for 'matches' with similar past experiences and associated emotions. It could find:

- a painful personal experience of redundancy
- knowledge that this person still has family responsibilities
- happy or frustrating experiences with this colleague at work
- vivid images of elderly people in hardship in recent films and TV documentaries
- my father's liberal philosophy
- recent knowledge of a company which was sunk by over-staffing
- feedback from colleagues who have complained of my 'over-sensitivity'
- a quote from a management guru on courageous leadership
- the religious teachings of my childhood which taught me to 'do as you would be done by' and 'respect for my elders'
- plus a good deal more equally confusing and contrasting material.

To make matters even more complicated, the personal screen through which I would view this choice would also be affected in part by my genetic inheritance (for example, my mother's 'sensitive' temperament and, probably, a cave ancestor's aversion to statistics!). And, in addition, it will be further influenced by my own innate driving needs (for example, possibly to be the leader of the pack) and my culturally acquired values (for example, centuries of British colonial arrogance!). What a mixture – no wonder I have now chosen to work as a sole-trader!

Our personal screen can be confused with intuition. This is because it often causes us to have a strong 'gut reaction' the moment we are faced with the problem – long before we may have had a chance to think it through.

If our personal screen has caused us to make the wrong decisions in the past (and it commonly does), we may then be sceptical of the very valid power of good intuitive thinking. This could be a great loss. Decisive people learn to rely on intuition more freely as they make more and more good choices.

So, how do gut reactions differ from intuition?

In short, gut reactions are prejudices (pre-formed judgements) while intuition is essentially a form of unconscious rapid thinking which is processed mainly on the right side of the brain. (Remember we discussed this earlier, back in Step 3.) You will be accessing your intuitive reasoning powers in Step 10 in our decision-making process.

We cannot escape the facts of our conditioning, genetic inheritance and underlying prejudices, but what we can do is look at them critically and honestly and then make attempts to counter their influence when we need and want to do so.

Some decisions obviously require us to be more objective than others. Should others be depending on us or paying us to make a rational and fair decision then we would have a responsibility to take extra care over this issue. I would expect a surgeon choosing whether or not to operate on me to be as objective as he or she can possibly be. But if friends were deciding whether or not to invite me to their wedding, I would want them to feel able to make an emotional and highly subjective choice.

So the kind of choice you are making will influence how much allowance you will make for your personal screen. (Sorry, that's yet another decision for you to make!)

> We cannot escape our 'inheritance', but we *can* look at it critically and honestly and then make attempts to counter its influence when we need to do so.

There are two distinct classes of what are called thoughts: those that we produce in ourselves by reflection and the act of thinking, and those that bolt into our mind of their own accord.

THOMAS PAINE

Action time!

- Write down your spontaneous 'gut reactions' to your problem.

- Confront honestly any possible personal prejudices you may have concerning any people involved in the situation. To do this you will have to re-examine your own driving needs and values. Perhaps the person is someone you love or hate, or someone from a cultural background or age group that is very different from your own.

- Note down any relevant past personal experiences. These need not be necessarily the same situation – they may simply have stimulated similar feelings. (For instance, in the earlier example about whether or not to make a senior employee redundant, any experiences of being rejected or grief about a missed grandparent might be significant.)

- Ask yourself what would your father or mother (and/or other significant parent figures) have done or advised in this

situation? Even if they wouldn't have been likely to give direct advice on such a choice, it is often useful to think through what they could have said. Because the influence of their values and example pervades our unconscious at such an impressionable time, it can last throughout our lives. (But as we have noted before, once it is in our consciousness we can counter it if we choose to do so.)

- **Ask yourself what any of your personal heroes or heroines (i.e. people who inspire you) would have chosen to do.**

- **Review the influence of the culture of the country and town you were brought up in.** Think, for example, how differently someone who had a poverty-stricken childhood in a highly commercialized city might react to a risky financial choice, compared with someone who came from a privileged landowning family in a remote rural village.

- **Think about the impact of any current influences on your subconscious mind.** For example:

- relevant advertising campaigns
- fashions and trends relating to your choice
- recent books/ films/ TV programmes which have had a powerful effect on you
- the culture of the company you work in or the community you live in

- **Summarize in four to six sentences the key potential influences on your choice of the above, starting each sentence in the following way:**

  'I need to be aware of and be in control of the potential influence of ...'

- **Look again at your gut reaction in the light of these sentences.**

The harder the choice, the more stressed you are likely to be. The more stressed you are, the more likely you are to be influenced by your pre-programmed mind. Aim to keep your 'inheritance' under your conscious control!

STEP 9

Examine and expand all your possibilities

Now it is time to look through your information folders that you compiled in Step 7 again. Your task at this stage is to examine the information you have gathered and then list as many of your options as you can. Once that has been done, each one will be critically examined first by you with your various thinking strengths (see Step 3), and secondly by others whom you choose to consult, especially by those you highlighted earlier who could be affected by your choice. (See page 71.)

I am aware that some of you will think that your options are already staring you in the face. You may indeed be feeling overwhelmed because you think that there are too many to handle.

Some of you could have the opposite kind of worry.

You might be feeling equally pressured because you feel cornered by having too few options.

I would suggest, however stark your choices appear to be, or whatever number you have to deal with, that you still work through this step. At the very least, you should find the exercises interesting and they may well prove useful for future decisions. You will also have an extra boost to your confidence, knowing that you have given your problem the very best examination that is currently in your power to give.

But another good reason for working through this step is that you may find some surprises! I know that these exercises have done this many times for me as well as for people with whom I have worked.

Finally, don't forget that you have the power to make this step as challenging as you dare it to be. **The more courageous you are in your consultations with others, the more rewarding your efforts are likely to be**. So be brave in your choice of people to consult. Most people are flattered to be asked their opinion – even busy, successful people and those with whom you may have little in common.

Information becomes knowledge
when it is relevant to circumstance.
In other words, if you can marry
data to a decision, it becomes
knowledge ... the key to surviving
under the avalanche of information
today is application not volume.

LOU ANN SMITH

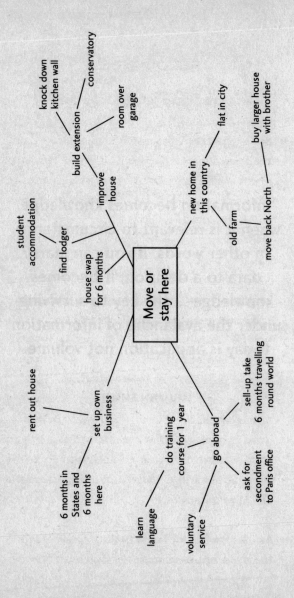

Action time!

• **Make a new folder labelled 'Options'.**

• **Set a deadline time which is challenging but realistic for completing this step.** This step needs a deadline more than most because the examination of options *could* last your lifetime! You may want to skim read the following exercises before setting your date.

• **Start noting down your options as they pop into your head or when you review the information you have in your files** (which you collated in Step 7). You could set these out in the form of a Mind Map® as illustrated on the opposite page. This is always the way that I start. I find that it quickly brings up new ideas for me, but if you are a more logical thinker, a more conventional list in a linear form may work better. (If you want to know more about Mind Maps® read Tony Buzan's *The Mind Map Book*.)

• **Ask a number of friends and/or colleagues to have a brainstorming session with you.** To do this, take a large piece of paper and write one word to represent your problem or dilemma in the centre of the page. Ask everyone to come up with as many ideas as they can. It does not matter how absurd they may sound. Jot these down around your central word without discussing them. When the pool of ideas has run dry, stand back and reflect. Add the best to your list of options.

• **Discuss your problem and list of options with as many different people as you can, including the people who could be affected by your choice**. Ask them for additions. If you can't meet up personally with people, consult them via post or email – but don't forget to give them a deadline time. Before adding others' options, consider the personal screens (which we discussed in Step 8) through which your 'consultants' may be viewing your problem.

• **Re-read your list of core values and the life-direction exercise you did in Step 2.**

- **Write a list of 'Musts' (i.e. your needs) in relation to your choice.** For example: *'It must make me happy'* / *'It must not give unnecessary hurt to anyone'* / *'It must not lose money'* and so forth.

- **Write a list of 'Bonuses' in relation to your choice** (i.e. your wants – the outcomes you'd like, but don't absolutely need). For example: *'It would be great if my choice pleased ___'* / *'It would be great if I became a millionaire'* / *'It would be great if we all agree'* and so forth.

- **Write a list of your main 'Fears' should your choice prove to be wrong.** You will need to look at the risk factor of each and the consequences should the 'worst-case' scenario befall you. For example: *'I may lose my job or chances of promotion'* / *'___ won't like me'* / *'I may not pass the exam'* / *'I may lose a customer'* / *'I may become physically ill/hurt'* and so forth.

- **Draw three columns at the side of your Mind Map® or list of options.** Head one 'Musts' and another 'Bonuses' and give each option a grading on a scale of 1–10 according to their ability to satisfy your needs or wants (10 for an excellent chance and 1 for a poor chance). Head your third column 'Fears' and grade accordingly (10 for the least likelihood of realizing your fear, and 1 for those which are most likely to do so). Remember to consider ways in which you could minimize the risk of each option or recover from failure before giving a grade. Now put your list aside and we will come back to it again in Step 10.

- **Take a break!** You deserve it and so does your choice. So relax and, at the very least, do something completely different for a short while before reading on.

STEP 10

Scale down to two alternatives

Did you take your break?

I hope so, because scaling down is perhaps the hardest work of all. It requires you to perform at your *very* best.

It's easy to panic at this stage. Crunch time is so obviously approaching. This is when minds are most likely to 'freeze', or we find it very tempting to push the decision onto the backburner or hand it over to someone else. To counter these kinds of self-sabotaging habits, you must now 'rev up a gear'. Be determined to keep active and stay positive. It will help you to do this if you mark your choice as high priority on your weekly 'To Do' list.

Now it's time to 'REV UP A GEAR'!

It is now also time to stop talking to the cynics and sceptics about your problem. In fact, try to spend most of your time with positive people who help to boost your self-esteem and confidence. Be assertive – say why you are being selective about the people you need around you – that way some of the cynics *may* transform themselves and become quite helpful!

You will be doing your scaling-down work in two stages. First, you will be reducing down your list of options to approximately six. I am assuming you now have more options than this – if you don't, you could still find it enlightening to do these exercises with the number you have – even if you only have two.

Secondly, you will be doing some exercises to help you to 'weed' your options down until you have only two left to choose between.

**When I need to make a decision,
I spend quite a lot of time
just wandering around, talking
to smart people.**

NEIL HOLLOWAY,
MANAGING DIRECTOR, MICROSOFT

Action time!

- **Look at the last exercise you did on 'Musts'/'Bonuses'/Fears** (see pages 91–2). Taking note of the grades in each of the columns, create a list of your six top options.

- **Use your imagination to bring the potential outcome of each one of these options to life.** First, make sure that you are physically relaxed and in a quiet environment. To bring your various possible outcomes alive, look at each in turn using the classic method of considering these famous six questions:

Who	– will be involved and who will be affected most?
What	– could happen?
Where	– will the outcome occur?
Why	– will it be useful, appropriate or pleasurable?
When	– will it take place?
How	– will it happen?

- **Close your eyes and run a mental 'movie' in your head of each potential outcome.** (Remember how to do it? If not, turn to pages 16–17.) Note down your feelings as you experience each of these outcomes. Do you need to keep considering the options that left you feeling bad or indifferent? If not, cross out these from your list.

- **Reflect on the outcomes you visualized and note also how in tune the outcome was with your core values and life-dream** (see Step 2). Can you cross out those from your list which do not meet this test?

- **Take a sounding on each option from a select group of no more than a few positive friends or trusted colleagues or mentors.** (You should by now know who is likely to be of most help.) After doing this, you can probably cross out at least one other.

- **If you have the inclination, and a willing friend or two, try your hand at acting.** Test out how you feel about some of your options by playing through scenes of possible outcomes.

(I did this with great success when I was trying to choose what to do when my first marriage was 'on the rocks'.) Only minimum acting skills are required and everyone has these, however deeply they are now buried. (Remember yourself as a toddler?)

- **Use your dream-power to help you think.** Read your list of options just before going to sleep. Set your alarm early so you can have some time when you wake to note down and reflect on your dreams. You may find, as I often do, that doing this clarifies the picture. But it's never a good idea to rely entirely on your dreams to guide your decision-making. Their 'insights' are often highly 'contaminated' by your feelings and the random 'clutter' your subconscious has picked up the previous day. The ideas they generate should always be checked out by conscious logical thinking and appraisal.

- **If you haven't already reduced your options to two – do so NOW!**

You should never exclude how you feel – or how you think other people might feel – from your decision-making process. But the most important first step towards making a tough decision is to think through your various choices and then relate them to your strategy.

TAMARA INGRAM, EXECUTIVE CHAIRMAN, SAATCHI & SAATCHI

Stage Four

make your final choice

This is the stage you have no doubt been waiting for! And I assure you the wait will prove to have been worthwhile. You should glide fairly effortlessly through these next two steps.

The first step will guide you through the process of making your final choice. And the second will show you how you can prepare an efficient contingency plan just in case the process of putting your choice into action doesn't go the way it should or as smoothly as you hoped.

STEP 11

Countdown to number one

The good news is that you have already done almost all of the groundwork there is to do. You are now ready to choose.

After all the other more sophisticated thinking you have done, the next two exercises may seem very simplistic. This is because they are! You might even call them the 'blunt instruments' of decision-making. They can indeed be dangerous in unprepared hands. But assuming you have diligently done all the previous exercises, yours are not. You need these simple tools *now* because they work, and they work fast! They will 'force' you to make your final choice cleanly and speedily.

So, the winning post is now in sight! I hope you feel both confident and excited! You should because you are about to make the best choice you could possibly make – at *this* point in time.

For those of you who are still trembling, remind yourself that we rarely ever feel *fully* ready to make a hard choice. Part of you will always yearn for more time. If you have read this book this far, this decision is obviously of great significance to you. This means that you *could* quite possibly devote a whole lifetime to it and still not choose. (It has been known! Deathbeds are notorious for bringing up such regrets.)

Enough said – let's get on with the action. But first make sure that you have:

- a coin
- red, orange/amber and green coloured marker pens
- two large sheets of paper

> **The winning post is now in sight, so it's time to make your final choice.**

**Nothing is more difficult, or
therefore more precious, than
the ability to decide.**

NAPOLEON BONAPARTE

Action time!

- **Take your coin and make one of your options heads and the other tails.** (Yes, I am serious!) Flip the coin NOW! Did your coin fall head-side up or tail-side up? Note the feelings this result has brought up – in particular the negative ones. These could, for example, be fear or sadness at losing an opportunity or a person.

  You may now be relieved to hear that you are not necessarily going to do what the coin told you to do! But remember how you felt after it was spun because you will need to take these feelings into consideration when making your final choice and writing your action plan later.

- **Take two sheets of paper – one for each option.** Divide each into two columns and mark them '**Pros**' and '**Cons**'. Working as fast as you can, fill in the columns for both options.

  When you have run dry of ideas, take one green, one orange/amber and one red marker pen (i.e. traffic light colours!). Mark each 'Pro' and each 'Con' as either:

Important (green),
or
Significant (orange/amber),
or
Insignificant (red)

The colourful prioritized lists which now face
you on the page should be making it 'blind-
ingly obvious' which route is right for you
to take.

SO MAKE YOUR FINAL CHOICE – **NOW!**

Relax for a few minutes, but *don't* celebrate.
(That comes later!) First you need to make
your contingency plan.

STEP 12

Make your contingency plan

This is another of the unsung secrets of great decision-makers. Lesser mortals often get this far and then start to panic yet again. The tortuous self-questioning starts:

'Have I made the right choice after all?'

'What will happen if …?'

They may even torture other people by repeatedly asking them these questions as well!

If you have ever met someone like this, you know how tempting it is to lose patience with them. You would be forgiven by many for strapping·them to the 'bed' they have just made for themselves and walking away!

Those of you who have done this to yourself must also know how utterly stupid this kind of self-defeating behaviour can make you feel. (I remember it well!)

This is why you need to make a contingency plan now. This will give you a ready-made action strategy to use if anything should go wrong as you are following through with your choice. If you adopt a 'wait and see' outlook and think you can 'cross that bridge' should you come to it, you may waste energy on needless worry and could even find yourself sliding straight back to where you were when you first picked up this book. Even if you do still stick with your choice – you will certainly not be in the best of moods in which to celebrate in the style you deserve!

Less commonly, there are people who don't tend to panic at this point, but run into danger by doing the opposite. They become over-excited. The rush of relief at making their choice gives them an emotional 'high'. You may have met them as well. They are often unbearably positive. You may find them irritatingly complacent and over-eager. They will not contemplate anything but the very best of outcomes. However hard they may have worked at making their choice, they can set it up to fail by rushing headlong into unplanned action. In this state of emotional blindness they may not notice the warning signs that are indicating that trouble is just around the corner. Then (even more irritatingly!) when they do get into trouble, you might see them bin this book and hear them say: 'I don't know why I bothered.'

Great decision-makers are realists. They don't forget that choosing is *always* risky. So they ensure that their heads stay in control of their hearts even at this stage. And at this point, although the last thing they may *feel* like doing is looking at worst-case scenarios, they will make their contingency plans before celebrating or converting their choice into action.

I hope that answering the following 10 questions will make this horribly 'sensible' task a good deal easier to get down to.

> Great decision-makers are realists. They don't forget that choosing is *always* risky and they plan for contingencies accordingly.

**Hope for the best,
And prepare for the worst.**

PROVERB

Action time!

- **Write down answers to the following 10 questions for *each* of the setbacks, problems or catastrophes you might encounter.** File them somewhere safe. (Writing and filing are great ways to force worries out of your head.)

1. Where and when or with whom is this most likely to happen?
2. What might be the warning signs that could signal it is going to happen?
3. Which of my own particular personal strengths or skills can I depend on to help me in this situation?
4. What feelings am I likely to experience?
5. What can I do to take care of my emotional health?
6. Who could I turn to for the best emotional support?
7. Who might be the best person to give me practical help?
8. Where might I obtain any necessary resources, information or advice?
9. What would be the first positive step I would take on hearing or seeing any 'bad news'?

10. What other kinds of action could I take to rescue or cope with the situation?

I was about to step outside the illuminated envelope of fear and meticulous daydreaming into the hard-edged world of consequences. I knew that one action, one event, would entail another.

IAN MC EWAN, *ENDLESS LOVE*

Stage Five

stick by your choice with confidence

Just when you thought it was all over, you find there is more to do!

I know the feeling. How I would love to pass the buck on at this stage. It is hard enough making the choice without having to think about putting it into action. But the good news is that the first step in this stage will not require that you do that. It is about rewarding and celebrating your achievement. Hopefully after doing this your energies will be so renewed that you will be more willing to work through the next crucial three steps! These may not sound particularly exciting but they are 'make or break' steps. After all, there is little point in making a brilliant decision if we sabotage its success by not following it up with equally brilliant action! So the second step in this stage will guide you through the process of writing an effective action plan. The third step will help you to communicate your decision assertively, and the final step will show you how you can monitor and evaluate your progress as you put your choice into action.

STEP 13

Reward yourself and celebrate your decision

Other than brain surgery, tampering with genes or administering potent pills, rewarding 'good behaviour' is *the* most powerful tool available to man for moulding personality – even our own! But how often do you use it? Not often enough, I guess. (You'd have to be pretty unusual if you did!)

I'm sure you would agree that making the very best of a hard choice is certainly behaviour worthy of recognition, not to mention a bonus. **By reinforcing this good decision-making behaviour with a reward and a celebration, you will be setting it on the road to fast becoming the kind of habit that you never want to lose.** Just think of how much time and energy such a habit would bring you in the future and how much more self-respect it will bring.

But it is unlikely that you'll be the only one to benefit. Habitually decisive people are great to have around. You must know yourself how they inspire confidence and motivation. As one of their number, you will undoubtedly grow in popularity! You should not be short of offers to help you celebrate. Of course, there could be some minor exceptions. The embittered cynics and green-eyed monsters may be 'otherwise engaged', but who needs them at a party anyway!

Some of you may be thinking: '*But I can't reward myself or celebrate until I know that my choice has been* **proved** *to be the right one.*'

I can understand this kind of reasoning. It dogged my own (largely miserable!) life for years. Fortunately I have now learned to separate my 'good behaviour' from my outcomes. For many reasons (possibly out of your control) your choice may not give you the result you want – all the more reason to remind yourself that:

- it doesn't take much courage, care or consideration to make a decision that has no risk
  involved; courage and decision-making skills

are worthy of recognition in their own right
- rewards and celebrations put us in a positive
  mood which means that we are much more
  likely to follow-up our choice with constructive,
  helpful behaviour.

Celebration is good for you and for your choice – so do it in style!

There is an applause superior to that of a multitude – one's own.

ELIZABETH ELTON SMITH 1836

Action time!

- **Reflect on how you felt before you started working so constructively and carefully on making your choice.** Compare these feelings to your emotional state now. Enjoy the difference!

- **Indulge yourself in some high-quality physical relaxation and self-nurturing activity.** Buy some especially nutritious and delicious food. Your body has been under some stress and will benefit from a spell of super-nourishment.

- **Give your mind some 'free time'.** Allow it the freedom to 'float' and feed it some luxury 'mind-food'. For some this might be a trip to the cinema to see a Sci Fi thriller or a romantic comedy; for others it might be a weighty autobiography or a visit to an antique fair or contemporary art show. It doesn't matter what it is you choose as long as what you are doing doesn't feel like a 'must' or a 'should' but more like a mental extravaganza!

- **Ring or email a friend or two and tell them you have made your choice.** Make sure that they are the kind of friends who you think will be pleased for you. If anyone starts querying your decision, just tell them firmly that you don't want to know! Repeat (as many times as you need to!): *'I have made my choice and now I simply want to celebrate my achievement in doing so.'*

- **Find an enticing way of celebrating – even if this seems like a minor activity such as going out for a drink with a friend, talking over the phone or chatting electronically.** Match your 'event' to the degree of importance the choice had for *you* – even if you know it may be viewed very differently by others.

- **If you can't find anyone free to celebrate at the moment, give yourself a big treat.** (Why not book that holiday you have always dreamed of?) Or try telling a stranger. For example, when the next person in a shop says *'Have a good day'* reply with: *'I am – I've just made a very hard choice and I feel so relieved.'* Believe me, the vast majority of people will respond in a very rewarding way.

STEP 14

Write your action plan

Beware – you are entering another danger zone!

When the celebrating is over and the cold light of day strikes, panic could strike once again. Perhaps you might recognize this kind of accompanying mental self-talk:

'Oh dear, what have I done?'
'Will I ever be able to go through with it?'
'What will ___ say? I don't know if I can face them.'
'Can I really afford it?'
'Suppose it is harder than I thought?'

So be ready with your pen and pad to fight off this self-defeating 'rubbish'. (Isn't that what it deserves to be called?!) You are about to start planning how to put your choice into effective action. This logical activity will soon defeat any sabotaging worries popping up from the right side of your emotional brain.

But even if you haven't woken up with the blues, your choice will benefit from the following action points. Hard choices may be difficult to make, but putting them into practice can sometimes be even harder! This is especially so should they require a major life change or you think they may involve upsetting someone. (And many, of course, necessitate both!)

If your difficult choice was a business decision, you shouldn't need convincing of the importance of a well-planned strategy after making a hard choice. You may already be one step ahead of us!

A well-planned strategy makes a hard choice easier to put into practice.

There is only one proof of ability: action

MARIE VON EBNER ESCHENBACH

Action time!

- **List or brainstorm the things you need to do now that you have made your choice.** (Forgotten how to? See the brainstorming exercise in Step 9.)

- **Mark each according to the priority rating they need.** (Your red, orange/amber and green coloured marker pens that you used in Step 11 could come in handy once again for highlighting their ranking order.)

- **Group suitable tasks together** (for example, purchases for one mega-shopping trip or phone calls for one sitting at your desk).

- **Set at least three dated step-by-step goals for yourself at suitably spaced intervals.** Make sure that the first of these is fairly immediate and the last is an achievable deadline. (For example, a long-term project might have a deadline for a week's time; another for three months' time, and the final date set for six months' time.)

- **Allocate the specific tasks you have identified to one of the above time periods.** Enter them into your diary with a coloured pen or use a special marker if you are working electronically. Doing this will enable you to keep better track of your progress.

STEP 15

Communicate your choice assertively to others

This task has a step all of its own because it is, in my experience, so often over-looked. After making a hard choice we are often too excited, too fearful or just too plain busy to be as thoughtful about others' needs as we would like to be. It is very rare for these kinds of decisions not to need some kind of a 'communication strategy'. Some may even require a team effort to make sure that the action you have just planned happens. Others may just require polite notification.

You will need to ensure your assertive skills are in good working order when you are setting out to communicate your choice to others. Hard choices, as we have seen already, usually involve change, and a risky change at that. So you can usually expect to meet some resistance. You may be surprised even at how much you will receive and the direction from which you may receive it. When 'push comes to shove', those closest to us may be the people least likely to want us or our lives to change. (And, ironically, they may have been the ones who were most keen for you to make up your mind!) You may find them directly or indirectly making the life of your action plan more difficult than it needs to be. This may not be because they love you any less. Their resistance may be fuelled by concern. Remember they may not have all the information you had which helped you to make your choice. Or they could simply be a little less adventurous by nature than you are.

In the world of work, resistance is similarly common. But there the reasons could be different. Even the people who should stand to benefit from your choice may try to get in your way. Beware – professional rivalry and personal envy that you have never seen before may start to come into play. Or you could find that people are simply not as willing as they previously indicated they might be to come up with the resources you need. Even though they may like your choice in principle, in practice they may be more concerned than you thought to cover their own financial backs or protect their own departments from extra pressure.

Sounds depressing? Of course. But aren't we better forewarned so we can forearm! Don't let yourself be discouraged now. Reinforce your right to stand by your carefully considered choice.

Communicate, communicate and communicate your choice! But don't forget that the style of your message is highly likely to affect the level of support you will receive from others.

The release of information to everybody concerned in the implementation of the decision is part of the decision-making procedure.

ROBERT HELLER

Action time!

- **Make a list of two or three people who could support you while you are making your choice happen.** Put them as fully in the picture as you can. The more they know about how hard this choice has been for you, the more committed they will be to giving you the moral or practical help you need.

- **Return to the list that you made in Step 7 of the people who are likely to be affected by your choice.** Note *how* you are going to communicate your decision to them. Remember, if your news is at all unwelcome, face-to-face communication is best. Use confident, reassuring body language. (For example, use a firm, even tone in your voice; relaxed but upright posture and direct eye contact whenever possible and appropriate.)

- **Acknowledge sympathetically people's diffi-cult feelings and the problems which might arise from your choice *without* being crawlingly over-apologetic.** (For example, prefacing your communication with a polite

'I appreciate that this may cause you some inconvenience ...' instead of 10 wimpishly delivered apologies littered throughout your speech!)

- **Give your message to the most important people on your list by at least two methods** (for example, a letter and a meeting, or a phone call and a card). These could be the people most affected by your decision or the people you most need to put it into effect.

- **Repeat your communication again, again and again – until you are absolutely sure your message gets through**. Research has shown that in times of change people rarely register the first communication!

STEP 16

Make regular progess checks

How tempting it is to put on the blindfold now and just get on with it, whatever the consequences. Even as I typed the heading 'Make regular progress checks' I could feel my resistance response rising. It was telling me that I sound so BORING!

Who wants to hear about this kind of stuff at the end of a book? The answer, of course, is no one.

But, nevertheless, I must write about it because I know what a difference regular progress checks have made to my own life. They have given me the courage to both persist with choices through diffi-cult circumstances and also to change my mind when I see that some have not proved to be right.

However, I still feel compelled to make this closing 'sermon' as brief as I possibly can. This is why I am ending it right now!

> You have a right to change your mind, but *only* do so if the future proves your choice to be wrong.

Example of a progress checklist

Is my choice:

- progressing at a good enough pace
- still making financial sense
- still maintaining a 70% chance of proving to be the right one
- not putting too much pressure on others
- giving me enough time to pursue my other goals
- staying in line with my life dream
- letting me keep my work/life balance
- feeding my need for adventure
- allowing me to stay fit and healthy
- stretching my potential

If you've truly committed yourself to something, given it everything you've got, and concluded that it is not for you – move onto something else ... each 'mistake' is an opportunity to learn, rendering it impossible to make a mistake.

SUSAN JEFFERS,
FEEL THE FEAR AND DO IT ANYWAY

Action time!

(The following should be done sooner rather than later!)

- Using your notes from your early work in this book on your values (see page 27) and the positive outcome you wanted from your choice (see page 96), compile a checklist similar to the example on page 135. It may help to consult interested parties before doing this.

- At regular intervals rate your progress against this checklist. (These could range from daily to yearly progress checks, depending on the type of choice you have made.)

- In some circumstances it is helpful to 'appoint' a monitor. This should be someone who can look at your progress objectively and who is able and willing to set aside time to support whatever you are trying to do. (If your choice has a life-threatening element to it or it involves you taking responsibility for others' welfare, a monitor would be essential.)

- **Take active notice of your evaluation.** Give yourself a reward when you are doing well. Take care of yourself when you are struggling and gather up all the learning you can reap from the mistakes you may make along the way.

A final word

I hope you have found the process of learning more about good decision-making worth the effort. If not, you may do so very soon! You should find the next hard choice you have to make a lot easier than the one you have just faced. If you have read this far you have probably acquired more wisdom than you think you have! So don't be fearful of having to 'go through it all again' should you need to do so soon. Seize the opportunity to start this strategy once again. Each time you use it, your decision-making will become easier. You should also notice it is becoming generally faster. It is then that you will begin to feel excited rather than daunted by the increase in quantity and complexity of the choices we have today. I used to think it would be heaven to live in a world where all the decisions were made for me. I hope you now agree that the reality is that that would be a living hell!

Enjoy your choices!

Further help

Recommended reading

Alan Barker, *How to Be a Better Decision Maker* (Kogan Page, 1996)

Tony Buzan, *The Mind Map Book* (BBC Consumer Publishing Books, 2000)

Roger Dawson, *The Confident Decision Maker* (Morrow, 1993)

Robert Heller, *Making Decisions* (Dorling and Kindersley, 1998)

Susan Jeffers, *Feel the Fear and Do It Anyway* (Arrow Books, 1987)

Gael Lindenfield, *Assert Yourself* (Thorsons, 1986)

___, *Super Confidence* (Thorsons, 1989)

___, *The Positive Woman* (Thorsons, 1992)

___, *Managing Anger* (Thorsons, 1993)

___, *Self Esteem* (Thorsons, 1995)

___, *Self Motivation* (Thorsons, 1996)

___, *Emotional Confidence* (Thorsons, 1997)

___, *Success from Setbacks* (Thorsons, 1999)

___, *Confident Children* (Thorsons, 2000)

___, *Confident Teens* (Thorsons, 2001)

___, *Shortcuts to Bouncing Back from Heartbreak* (Thorsons, 2002)

___, *Shortcuts to Getting a Life* (Thorsons, 2002)

Gael Lindenfield and Malcolm Vandenburg, *Positive Under Pressure* (Thorsons, 2000)

Richard Nelson-Jones, *Effective Thinking Skills* (Continuum International Publishing Group, 1996)

Anthony Robbins, *Awaken the Giant Within* (Pocket Books, 1992)

Lou Ann Smith, *Be Decisive!* (Change Your Life Books, 1999)

Cassettes

Gael Lindenfield has made a number of personal-development tapes. Each is designed as a self-help programme of exercises to be used on a regular basis. The list of titles includes:

Self Motivation (Thorsons, 1997)
Self Esteem (Thorsons, 1998)
Success from Setbacks (Thorsons, 1999)
Managing Emotions at Work (Thorsons, 1999)
Emotional Confidence (Thorsons, 2000)

These cassettes are available at all good book-shops, or direct from Thorsons (telephone 0870 900 2050 or 0141 306 3296).

About the author

You can contact Gael Lindenfield through her publishers at the following address:

Gael Lindenfield c/o Thorsons
HarperCollins*Publishers*
77–85 Fulham Palace Road
Hammersmith
London W6 8JB
United Kingdom

Or you can contact her directly by email:
lindenfield.office@btinternet.com

For further information about Gael Lindenfield and her current programme, go to her website:
www.gael-lindenfield.com